ANTHOLOGY
OF MUSICAL FORMS

Leon Stein

© 1962 (Renewed 1990) Summy-Birchard Company
division of Summy-Birchard Inc.
All Rights Assigned to and Controlled by Alfred Publishing Co., Inc.
All Rights Reserved including Public Performance. Printed in USA.
Library of Congress Catalog Card Number 62-12879
ISBN 0-87487-044-5

3 5 7 9 11 13 15 16 14 13 10 8 6 4 2

Summy-Birchard Inc.
exclusively distributed by
Alfred Publishing Co., Inc.

CONTENTS

PART II: ADDITIONAL SELECTIONS FOR ANALYSIS

INTRODUCTION

The ANTHOLOGY OF MUSICAL FORMS is intended as a supplementary source of reference material to STRUCTURE AND STYLE (Summy-Birchard Company,©1962). The music in the anthology is divided into two sections. In Part I (pages 5-131), each composition is classified in the category of the form which it exemplifies, the order of succession being correlated with the sequence of forms and procedures discussed in STRUCTURE AND STYLE. In some cases, where two examples of a form are shown, one composition is analyzed throughout. In other instances, the first portion of a composition is analyzed in order to provide a guide for further analysis. To facilitate class work, each composition is numbered every five measures. In Part II (pages 132-159), the compositions are not classified as to form. These may be used for additional assignments, examinations, or for general reference.

The following abbreviations may be used in analysis:

M. T.—Main theme

S. T. —Subordinate theme

Tr. —Transition

M. —Motive

C. M.— Contrary motion

‾‾‾‾‾‾V‾‾‾‾‾ to indicate phrase separation

‾‾‾‾‾‾|‾‾‾‾‾ to indicate an elided cadence

In periods, double periods, and phrase groups, lower case letters may be used to indicate melodic phrase-relationships. Thus, a parallel double period may be indicated by *a b a' c*; a phrase group of three different phrases by *a b c*, etc. In contrapuntal works and in the larger homophonic forms, capital letters may be used to identify motives and motive relationships, the same letter being used for a motive and for its variants. In the song forms and larger structures, capital letters or Roman numerals (Part I, etc.) may be used to designate principal divisions. In polyphonic forms, principal divisions will often be sections rather than parts, and may be so indicated (Section I, etc.).

As a basis for analysis and discussion, the student should identify or determine:

1. The length of each structural unit.
2. Key areas of phrases, periods, parts, sections, and larger divisions.
3. Important points of modulation.
4. The patterns of principal parts and of auxiliary members.
5. The relationships (similarities or differences) of the units of structure in terms of melody, harmony, rhythm, texture, color, and the use of specific figures or motives.
6. The distribution of tensions.
7. The idiom used (modal, tonal, duodecuple, etc.).
8. Adherence to or departure from the "norm" of the specific form.
9. Stylistic aspects which are characteristic of the period in which the work was written.
10. Stylistic aspects which are characteristic of the composer.
11. The general principles of structure which are illustrated, viz., unity, variety, balance, contrast, climax, consistency.
12. The expressive function of a progression or procedure.
13. The influence of any extra-musical association (text, title, program) on the form and content.
14. The objective of the work. Is it self-contained or is it a movement or division of some larger work? Is it an "abstract" or a subjective type?

In the main, the above points concern factual aspects. After these aspects are observed, identified, and explained, they must be correlated. For, unless and until the particulars revealed by analysis are reintegrated, the total concept of a work may be unperceived. It will therefore devolve upon the instructor to synthesize and unify details and relate the factual to the more abstract aspects of communication, meaning, and aesthetic value.

The student should play or at least manage to hear played every work assigned for analysis. Finally, before proceeding with analysis, it will prove helpful to review the section on *Techniques and procedures of analysis* (p. XIII) in STRUCTURE AND STYLE.

SONG FORMS

1. One-Part Song Form (Phrase)

Ex. a Chanson de Geste   11th century French melody

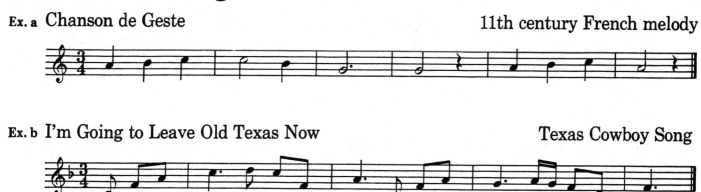

Ex. b I'm Going to Leave Old Texas Now   Texas Cowboy Song

2. One-Part Song Form (Period - a b)

Barbara Allen   Scotch Folk Song

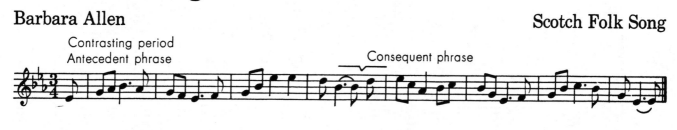

3. One-Part Song Form (Double Period - a a' a a")

Prelude, Op. 28, No. 7   Chopin

4. *Simple Two-Part Song Form* (A B)

5. *Expanded Two-Part Song Form* (A B)

Venetian Boat Song, Op. 19, No. 6

Mendelssohn

6. *Incipient Three-Part Song Form* (A B A)

Ex. a Old Folks at Home

Stephen Foster

Ex. b Symphony No. 9, Finale

Beethoven

For a third example, see the first sixteen measures of the Menuetto from Mozart's Serenade for String Orchestra, page 30.

7. *Three-Part Song Form* (A B A)

Ex. a Dedication (Widmung), Op. 25, No. 1 — Schumann

Con molto affetto

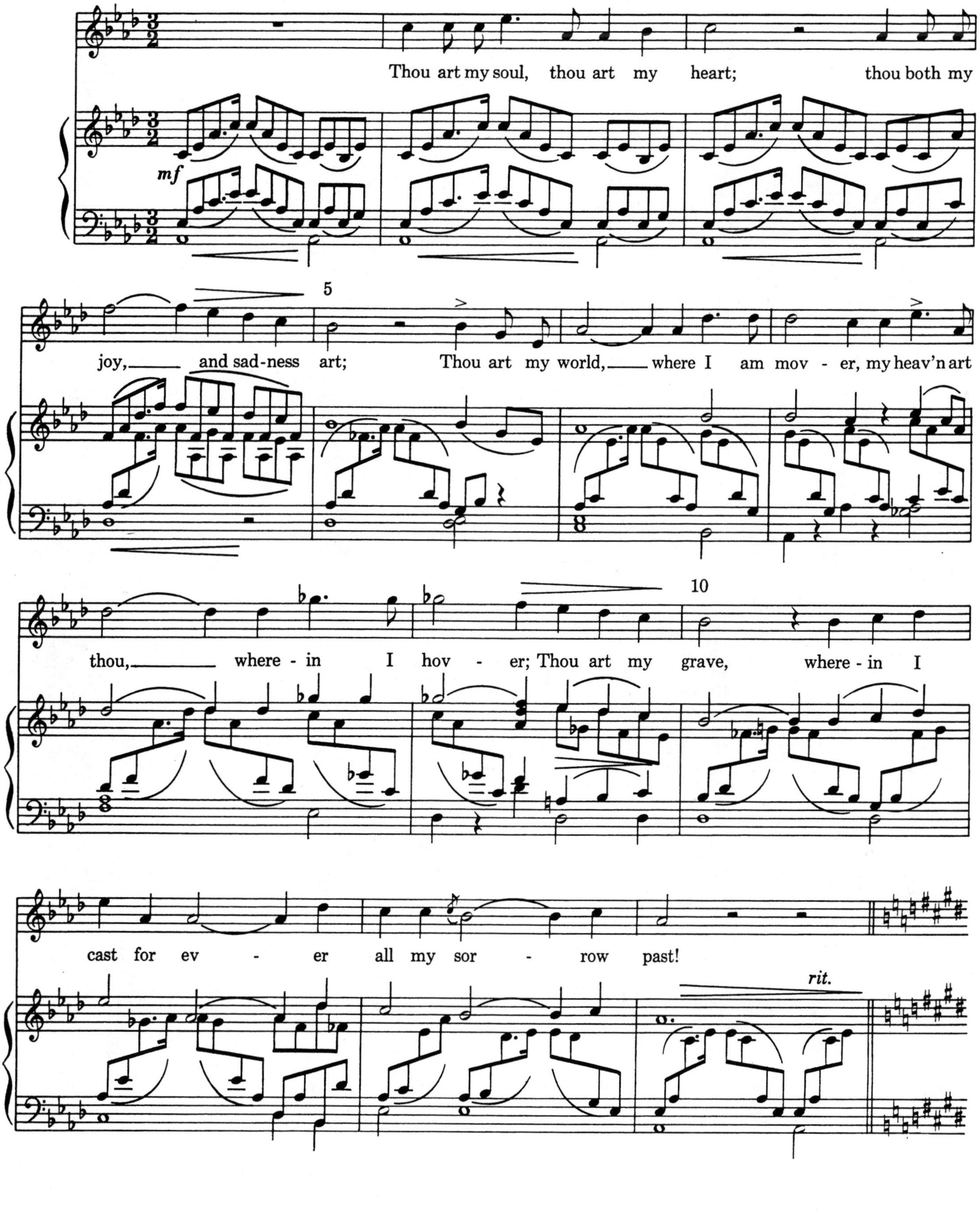

mf
Thou art my soul, thou art my heart; thou both my
5
joy, and sad-ness art; Thou art my world, where I am mov - er, my heav'n art
10
thou, where - in I hov - er; Thou art my grave, where - in I
cast for ev - er all my sor - row past!
rit.

Thou art my rest, my peace _____ pro - tect - ing

Thou art from Heav'n my life _____ di - rect - ing. Make me, by

worth, thy love to own! ___ Thy glance to me ___ my-self hath shown! ___ Thou'rt ever

round ___ me hov - 'ring by, My guar - dian sprite, my bet - ter

30

f

I!   Thou art my soul, thou art my heart;   Thou both my

35

joy____ and sadness art;   Thou art my world, ___ where I am mov - er, My heav'n art

thou, ___ where-in I hov - er, my guard-ian sprite, my bet - ter I!

p

40

rit.

Ex. b Beside the Cradle, Op. 68, No. 5

Grieg

8. *Enlarged Three-Part Song Form* (A B A B A)

Waltz, Op. 39, No. 15

Brahms

9. *Five-Part Song Form* (A B A B′ A)

Ex. a Spinning Song, Op. 67, No. 4

Mendelssohn

Ex. b Mazurka, Op. 7, No. 1

Chopin

10. Group Form (Ex. a - A B C) (Ex. b - A B A B C Coda)

Ex. a String Quartet in D Minor, 2nd movement (Theme)   Schubert

Ex. b The Rider's Song, Op. 68, No. 23

Schumann

11. Through-Composed Song (A B C D Coda)

Restless Love, Op.5, No.1

Schubert

Part III

Kro - ne des Le - bens, Glueck oh - ne Ruh', Lie - be bist

du, o Lie - be bist du, o Lie - - - -

- - - - - - - be,___ Lie - be bist du!

SINGLE-MOVEMENT FORMS

12. Song Form with Trio

Ex. a Serenade for String Orchestra, Menuetto

Mozart

A literal reduction of open score is often not playable. A close interpretation such as this provides an adequate version.

Trio   Three-part song form

Men.da capo

Ex. b Minuetto

A. Casella

Musette
Allegretto

Tempo I.

13. *First Rondo Form* (A B A)

Sonata, Op. 2, No. 1, second movement   Beethoven

M. T. (A) Incipient three-part song form
Part I Parallel period
Antecedent phrase

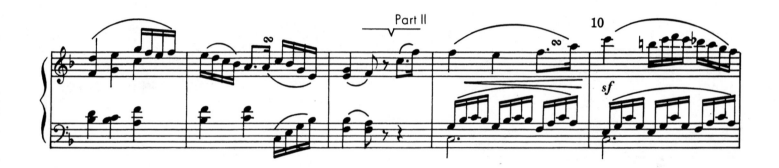

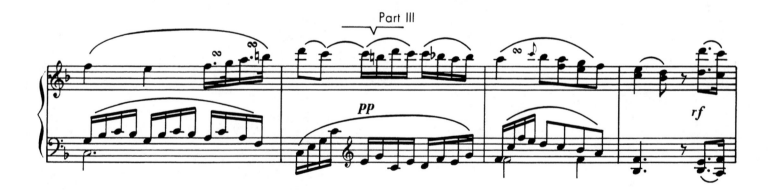

Whether as the result of conscious design or of subconscious thinking, the figure of the descending second dominates this whole movement. This figure is prominent in every measure and, with the exception of measure 27, in every cadence. At the end of each phrase, the first note of the descending figure is treated either as a suspension or as an appoggiatura in a delayed cadence. In measure 29, the descending second becomes the means of embellishing the scale passage of measure 27. A comparison of measures 27, 29, 54, and 56 indicates the progressively more complex embellishment of the descending second figure.

M. T. (A) Embellished return

14. Second Rondo Form (A B A C A)

Sonata in D Major, last movement

Haydn

15. *Third Rondo Form* (A B A C A B A)

Sonata, Op. 2, No. 3, last movement

Beethoven

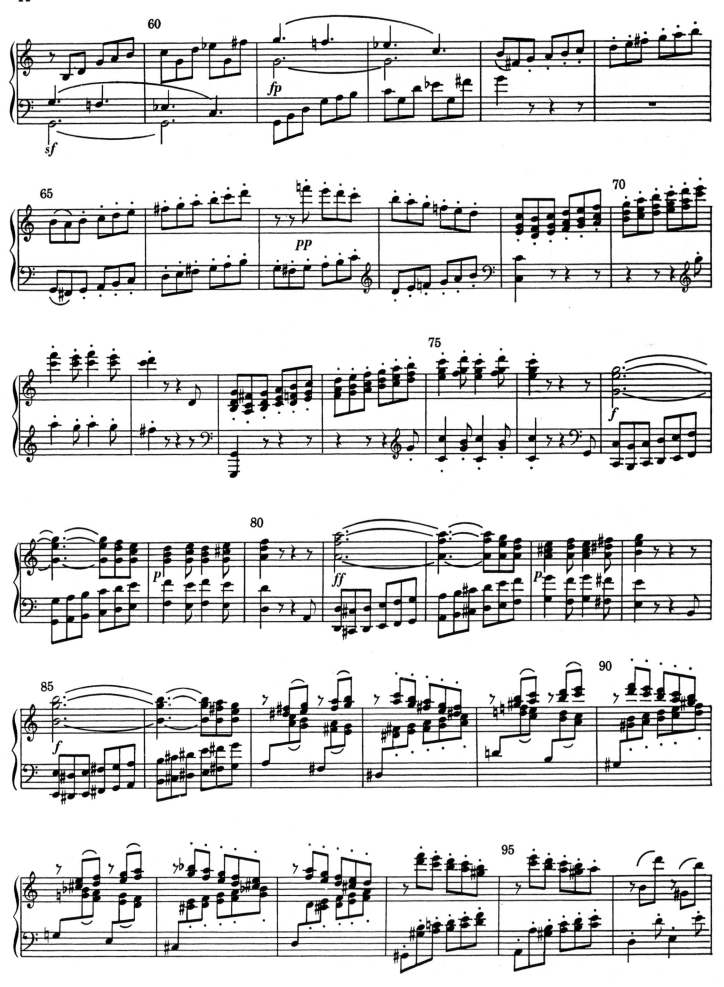

16. Variation Form

The theme is a single phrase of eight measures. Each variation (with the exception of No. 32) is eight measures in length ·and is based on the harmonies of the theme. An additional framework is provided by the melodic outline of the bass and treble parts:

Since the theme is in triple meter, in minor, eight measures in length, and essentially a series of harmonies, this set of variations is a Chaconne type. Only a selected number of the thirty-two variations are included here for analysis.

Thirty-two Variations on an Original Theme

Beethoven

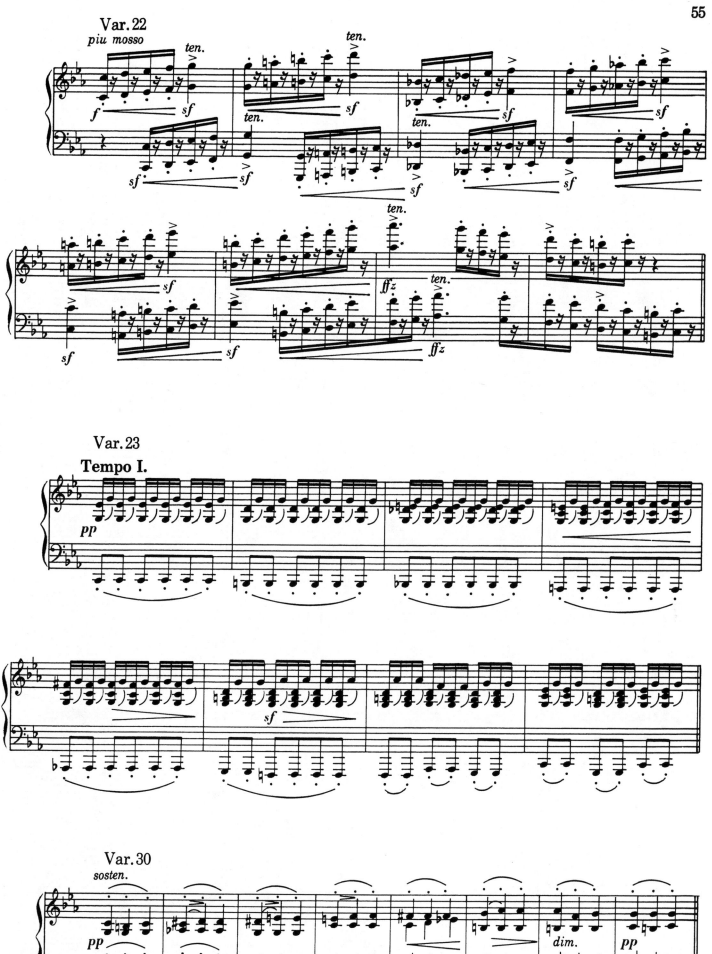

17. *Sonatine Form*

Ex. a Sonatina, Op. 20, No. 1, first movement

Kuhlau

Exposition
M. T.   Double Period

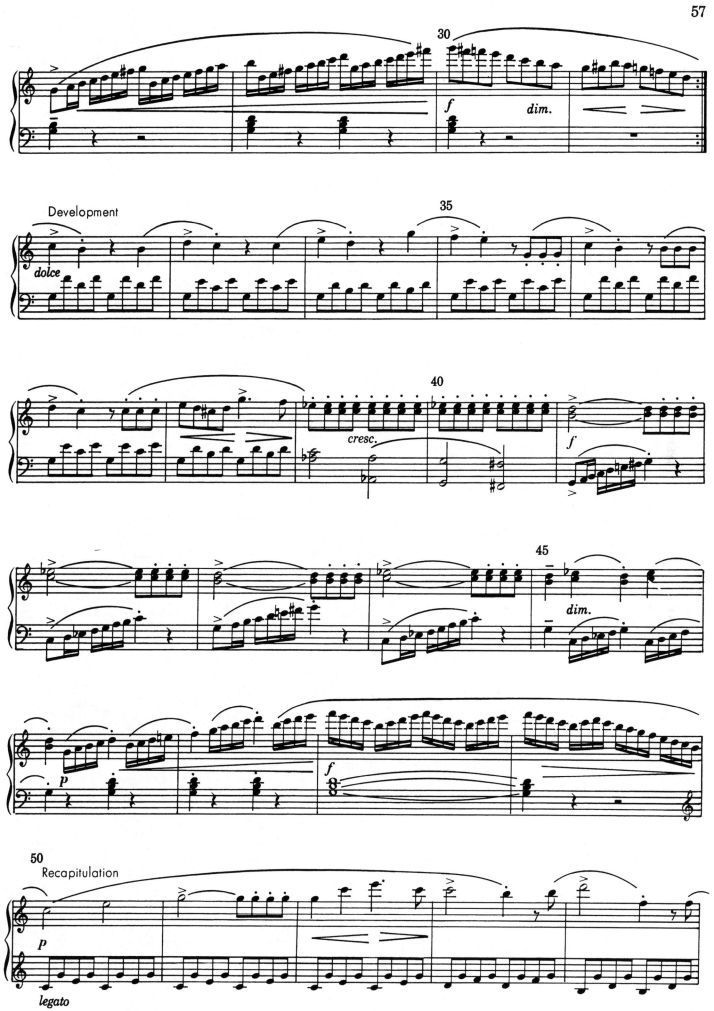

Ex. b Sonatina, No. 1, Op. 13, first movement

Kabalevsky

Note the arc form (Bogen form) of the main theme: Measures 1—2 3—4 5—6 7—8
                                                            a   b   b   a

Harmonic treatments illustrated in this movement are: pan-diatonicism (measures 1—8), modality —Aeolian mode with chromatic counterpoint (measures 32—35), parallel movement of triads (measures 88—91), shifting tonality (measures 129—134).

18. Single-movement pre-Classic sonata

Ex. a Binary form

Sonata in G major

Scarlatti

M.T. (transposed to dominant)

Ex. b Ternary form

Sonata in F minor

Scarlatti

19. Sonata-Allegro

Sonata, Op. 31, No. 3, first movement

Beethoven

CONTRAPUNTAL FORMS

20. Invention

Ex. a Two-voice Invention in C major   Bach

In the following example, the sections are:

Section	Measures	Begins in	Modulates through	Ends in
I	1−7	C major	G major	G major
II	7−15	G major	C major, D minor, A minor	A minor
III	15−22	A minor	D minor, C major, F major, C major, F major	C major

Measures 7−8−11−12−13−14 are the double counterpoint and transposition of measures 1−2−3−4−5−6. Section II is therefore Section I transposed and with two interpolated measures (measures 9−10). Measures 17−18 as a unit are a sequence of measures 15−16. In measures 19 and 20, the treble and bass parts are the contrary motion of the same parts in measures 3 and 4.

Ex. b Two-voice Invention in D minor

Bach

21. Fugue

Because of its individual character and importance, the counterpoint (alto voice, measures 3—4) may be termed thematic rather than merely accompanimental. Except for the last measures, every appearance of the subject (in whole or in part) is associated with this counterpoint. The following interrelationships are noteworthy:

1. The beginning of the subject (soprano, measure 11) is also a sequence, begun in measure 9. Similarly, the beginning of the subject (soprano, measure 20) is a sequence, begun in measure 19.
2. The soprano of measures 13—14 is the contrary motion of the bass of measures 10—11.
3. Measures 22—24 are the transposition of measure 9 through the first half of measure 11.
4. The material from the end of measure 26 through measure 28 is derived from measures 7—8. The counterpoint, originally in the soprano, is divided between the soprano and alto in measures 26—28.
5. The use of transposition (sometimes modified) and of triple counterpoint is illustrated in measures 7—8 from 3—4 (the alto in measures 7—8 being an added counterpoint); measures 15—16 from 7—8; measures 17—18 from 5—6; measure 19 from 18; measures 20—21 from 15—16.

Ex. a Fugue No. 2, Vol. I, Well-Tempered Clavier   Bach

Ex. b   Concerto Grosso VII, Op. 6, No. 7 (fugue)   Handel

The cembalo part of this fugue was not actually written by Handel, but is a realization for keyboard of the figured bass part.

86

22. Passacaglia

Ex. a   Passacaglia in C minor (excerpts)

Bach

Ex. b   Passacaglia from String Quartet No. 2   Bloch

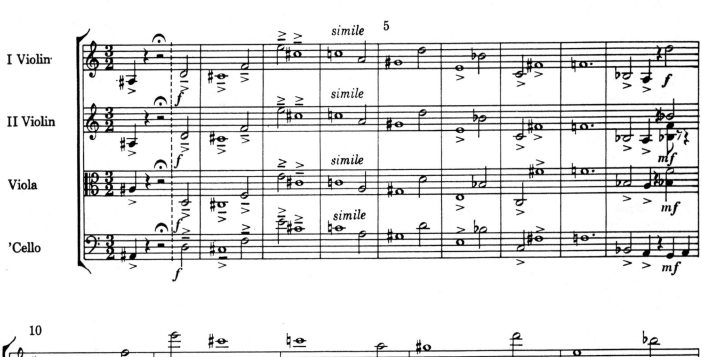

23. Toccata

Toccata Nona

A. Scarlatti

24. Chorale Prelude

Nun Danket Alle Gott (Now Thank We All Our God)

Bach

Organ

25. Baroque Suite

French Suite No. 6 (excerpts)

Bach

*Allemande

Allegro moderato

*Binary form with polyphonic texture and motivic treatment.

*Two-part song form with predominant top-line melody.

* Menuet

Moderato

*Three-part song form with predominant top-line melody.

*Gigue
Vivace

*Imitative treatment of a subject (invention type) in sectional form.

26. *Instrumental Canzona*

Faulte d'argent   Josquin des Pres

Falte D'Argens   Girolamo Cavazzoni

112

27. *Sixteenth-Century Motet*

Dies Sanctificatus   Palestrina

28. Free Forms

Ex. a Polyphonic Type

Prelude to Suite No. 8

Handel

The following example is an illustration of a free form which is based on motivic development. In this particular work, the principal devices used are imitation and sequence. There is no clear-cut cadence until the very last measure of the movement. Among the devices used to evade cadences are suspensions (soprano, measures 6 and 9), unexpected change of harmony (last beat, measure 18), and the continuous imitative or sequential treatment of the motives. Consequently, the sectional divisions are more tentative than factual; they suggest where terminal cadences *might have* occurred except for the evasions. No pre-established pattern is followed, nor is there any planned reutilization of material as in an invention or fugue. The total effect is that of an improvisation in a treatment similar to what, in twentieth-century literature, is termed a "stream of consciousness" technique. The total effect, too, is that of a work of surpassing beauty.

The principal motives are shown below. Since the contrary motion and simple variants of the motives are easily recognizable, the same letter is used for the original motive and its variants.

Ex. b Homophonic Type

Fantasy in D minor

Mozart

Ex. c Opera Prelude

Prelude to Lohengrin

Wagner

29. *Mosaic treatment of motives*

Symphony No. 4, first movement (excerpt)

Mahler

128

30. Tone-Row Technique

Following is the original series (and melodic variants) on which the Schönberg Phantasy, Op. 47, is based.

Phantasy for Violin

Schönberg

Additional selections for analysis

Gigue

C.P.E. Bach

Puck, Op. 71, No. 3

Grieg

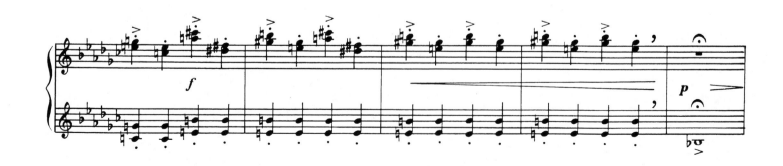

Game, From "For Children," Vol. I

Bartók

Moderato, From "The Five Fingers"

Stravinsky

Mississippi

Douglas Moore

Slow and sad

More lively

Slow and sad

Lively

Poeme, Op. 69, No. 1

Scriabine

Reverie

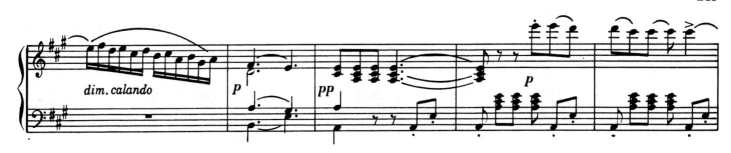

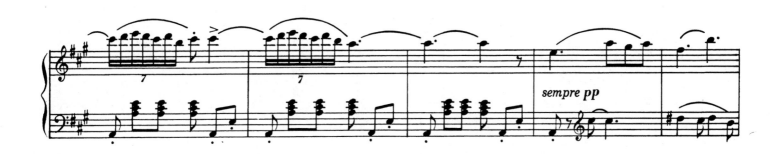

Sonata No. 34 (first movement)

Haydn

Allegro moderato

Symphony, Op. 21 (Variation movement)*

Webern

*Note: All instruments sound as written.

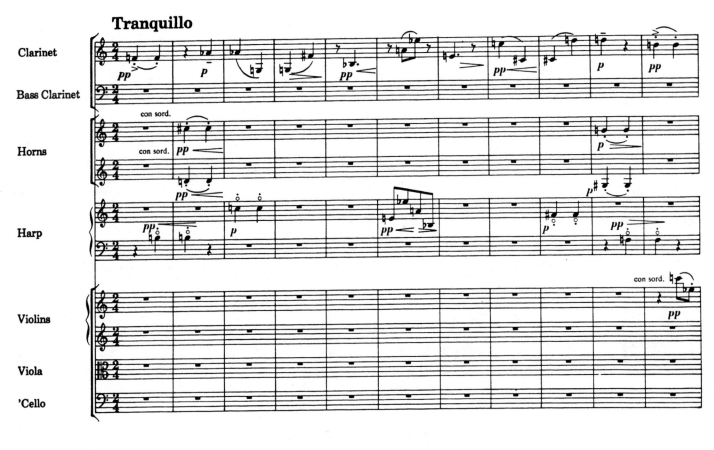

Var. 2
meno mosso

Prelude, Op. 34, No. 24

Shostakovich

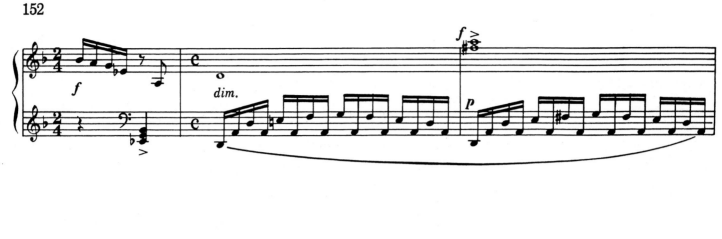

Mazurka, Op. 68, No. 3

Chopin

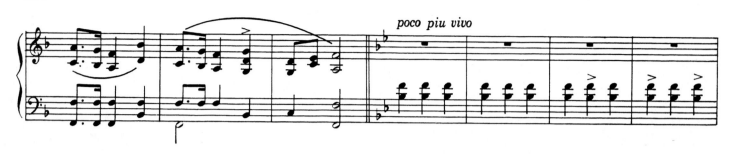

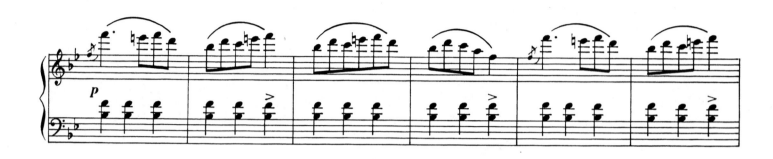

Sonata, Op. 49, No. 1

Beethoven

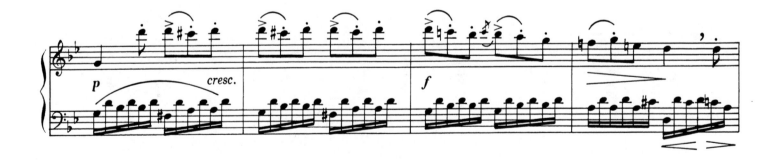

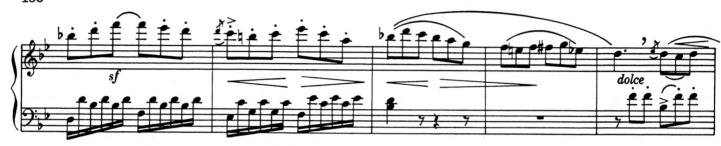

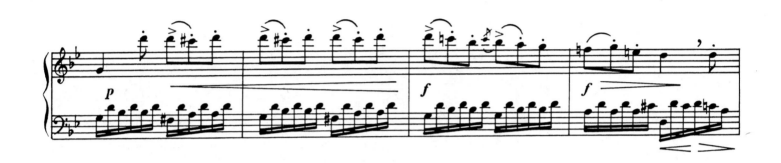

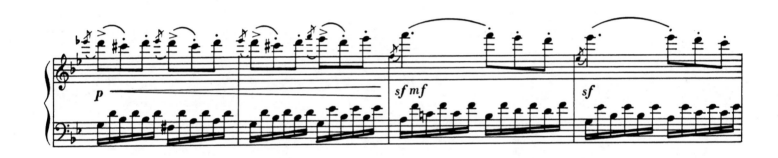